THE CAROUSEL OF LIFE

FORTY TALES THROUGH POETRY AND ART

BAHAREH AMIDI

Dedicated to my mother who has been with me on this carousel of life and who has been a mother to so many people riding the same carousel as I.

تقدیم به مادر عزیز و مهربانم
که برای همه مادر هستند.

INTRO BY...

Diane Harvey holds a PhD in Philosophy from Stanford University and is Professor Emeritus at Menlo College in California.

Dr. Harvey had the honor and pleasure of having Bahareh in her college courses and commends both Bahareh and her writings to the reader.

Bahareh Amidi shares a secret with you: that you are here to contribute something special, something unique, something that will use all of your skills, talents, and experiences. Like most of us, Bahareh suspected there was something more long before she figured out what it was for her. Like Siddhartha, Bahareh sought the answer to her uniqueness in the everyday world: she excelled at her studies, earning a PhD in Educational Psychology; she gave generously of her time and care in her relationships with her friends, her extended family, and her own family; she created a business that brought beauty into the homes of those who sought an aesthetic life; but the answer was not to be found in those pursuits; the answer was not where she expected it to be.

Carefully chronicling her journey, Bahareh began to explore life in a spiritual dimension. She wrestled with the age-old question of the relationship of the spiritual world to the everyday world. She began to understand that her contribution would only begin when she honored her own gifts, rather than seeking worldly success, when she stopped seeking on her own terms and accepted what came to her. One day, Bahareh came to realize that the journals that she had kept were not about the contribution she sought to make; they were the contribution. Bahareh, the poet had come to be.

Whether reading or listening to Bahareh's poetry, you will find yourself experiencing the world from a different perspective. Let Bahareh share her journey with you as you find your own unique way of contributing to the world, your own perspective. After all, you both know that you are here to contribute something unique.

Have you ever stood under a starless sky and watched the constellations forming before your eyes simply in your thoughts? Have you ever entered a concert hall full of instruments and empty of musicians and performers and herein listened to the most magnificent music of your heart?

The Carousel of Life is this real and magical space. The space between each wink of an eye. The gap between a breath in and a breath out, as you swim in the desert and fly under the sea with a school of fish rainbow colored.

This book is the universal stories waiting to be told. This book is the bridge between East and West. The bridge between genders, colors, and religions.

Simply, a bridge held suspended in time and space. Here. Now. This book is a mirror for you to look within and look ahead.

Welcome to The Carousel of Life.

Bahareh

June 3
10:00 am. 2015
Starbucks Kiawah
Hannah-mo

— Book Summary —

Have you ever stood under a starless sky and watched the constellations forming before your eyes simply in your thoughts? Have you ever entered a concert hall — full of instruments and empty of musicians and performers and here in listened to the most magnificent music of your heart.

The Carousel of life is this real and magical space. The space between each wink of an eye — The gap between a breath in and a breath out as you swim in the desert and fly under the sea with a school of fish rainbow colored.

This book is the universal stories waiting to be told.

This book is the bridge between East + West. The bridge between genders, colors and Religions. A bridge held suspended in time + space — Here slow. This Book is a mirror for you to look within and look ahead to the Welcome to the Carousel of life

CHARLIE DAVOLI / IN SEARCH OF LOST TIME / 2015

THE ANGEL WHO LOST HIS WINGS

Once upon a time
there was an Angel
an Angel who had lost his wings
he was walking through life
wondering what fault had made his wings disappear
he saw the birds flying through the sky
and the bees buzzing around
he saw a rock by the river and
he sat
and sat
and sat
after years of sitting
he decided
to walk again and look for his wings
that is when he started to fly wingless
with heart

BEYOND THE BRIDGE

Beyond the bridge is where
I know I have sat before

Beyond the bridge is where
I have drunk before

Beyond the bridge was where
I used to wear a mask

and play games with others who wore
a few layers of masks

Now as I sit at the banquet with
the snails who have arrived
from a pilgrimage within

I realize that there is no maze and no
labyrinth if one is in search of light

MOHSEN KASIROSSAFAR / PONTE / 2013

LOOKING AT MY SAME LIFE WITH NEW EYES

When I pretend to look I stop seeing

There are waves in the ocean with no sound

I breathe in but with every breath out I release more uncertainty and more doubt

The breeze felt by the corpse

by the white bird and on my skin

The truth held in the breeze

The truth can be warm and beautiful

The breeze today is daunting but not frightening

It is the same sea I walked in last year
The same shore I marked with my footsteps
with my dreams and doubts
But today with every step my foot goes in twice as deep as last year
but comes out with ease
What is the truth in my heavy step
Is it all that I have collected in my heart
or all that I've released from the web of lies that gives me this weight
Still in search but now I feel each and every step
each and every breath

THE SOUNDLESS CLAPPING HANDS

Listen to the heartless soul

there is no joy

there is no cry

if you cry without a sound

and if you are joyous without clapping

you are not adding life

to the universe

THE SILVER STREAM OF TRUTH

I imagine the milky way in a starless night
I imagine a school of fish in a sea with no water
I imagine myself floating in this space called life with no body weighing me down

If I were an invisible bit of fairy dust
in the story of not Peter Pan but the story of Bahareh's spring
Would I be able to fill all the springs of the universe with fairy dust
Or better yet let me remain a speck of dust
and visit people from shoulder to shoulder

I would spend some time in the dark mines where people are trying to find themselves
I would then spend some time in the mines
where people spend lifetimes trying to find gold
The gold is easy to recognize it shines
Those who excavate inside when do they know the truth

There are so many hearts to visit as a speck of fairy dust
I would love to be in the heart of a dog
and get to know its gentle truth as man's best friend
Are we really deserving of such generous love
The seeing dog helps guide me along

Here on this vessel carrying men and women
I see three men sitting in their own compartment
One is a man of God reading the Quran for safe travels
The other is a man of God reading the Bible hoping for another resurrection
And the third man holds a Torah and knows he sees God
Even as I sit on each of their shoulders I do not understand why
Why would the first kill the second
and the second slaughter the third all in the name of God
I would like to remain here a while to find out why

I spend some time in an orphanage
There are five boys and five girls
A man they call uncle who pays for their care
The woman they call house mother is blood related to one of the girls
The one girl has a mother but the rest have never felt the touch of theirs
They sleep at night dreaming and wondering what it would be like
I can never know
but for now each night I will hold each one tight

I continue down the lane to a mansion
filled with things and one old man and lots of maids
The old man has never seen the face of his children
since they walked out years ago after a quarrel over money
He sits counting his teeth in the mirror
and he notices love as a speck of dust on his shoulder
I see a teardrop and I disappear to another place and time

Now that I can perform this magic
I want to remain a speck of dust and travel in myself
get to know each twist and curve
and see if I might find more of me that I do not know

Please hold my hand
don't let me go
I am not afraid of you letting me go
These days I do not think I am afraid at all
It just seems to me that I need your company
As I breathe in this feeling and breathe out the questions of why

Now that I am back in the desert
I realize I never have to pretend to be a speck of dust
In reality I am never anything but a speck of dust
The more I see my smallness
The closer I feel to you

PURPLE HUES I IMAGINE AT NIGHT

The seagulls have come to the gate from which I shall depart
They have come to remind me of the simplicity of flight and the simplicity of sight
There is one lone black sparrow
her message is a bit different
She wants me to know I am loved and I should not be scared
I have done no wrong
every flight will have some peaks and some valleys
I sit now on a branch called life
Along the way I have met such nice birds
Some with wings some with sight
Some with no hands but with big open palms
There have been the ones with a stone for a heart
but even those have helped me bridge my colors and hues and shades of no color to purple

PIERRE SCHMIDT / RESSENTIMENT I / 2014

THE DETACHED HEAD

The neck that carried the head
on the body of the unmerciful
was tired
it would rather be detached
with the possibility of being found by a grateful soul
The head lies on the field in anticipation

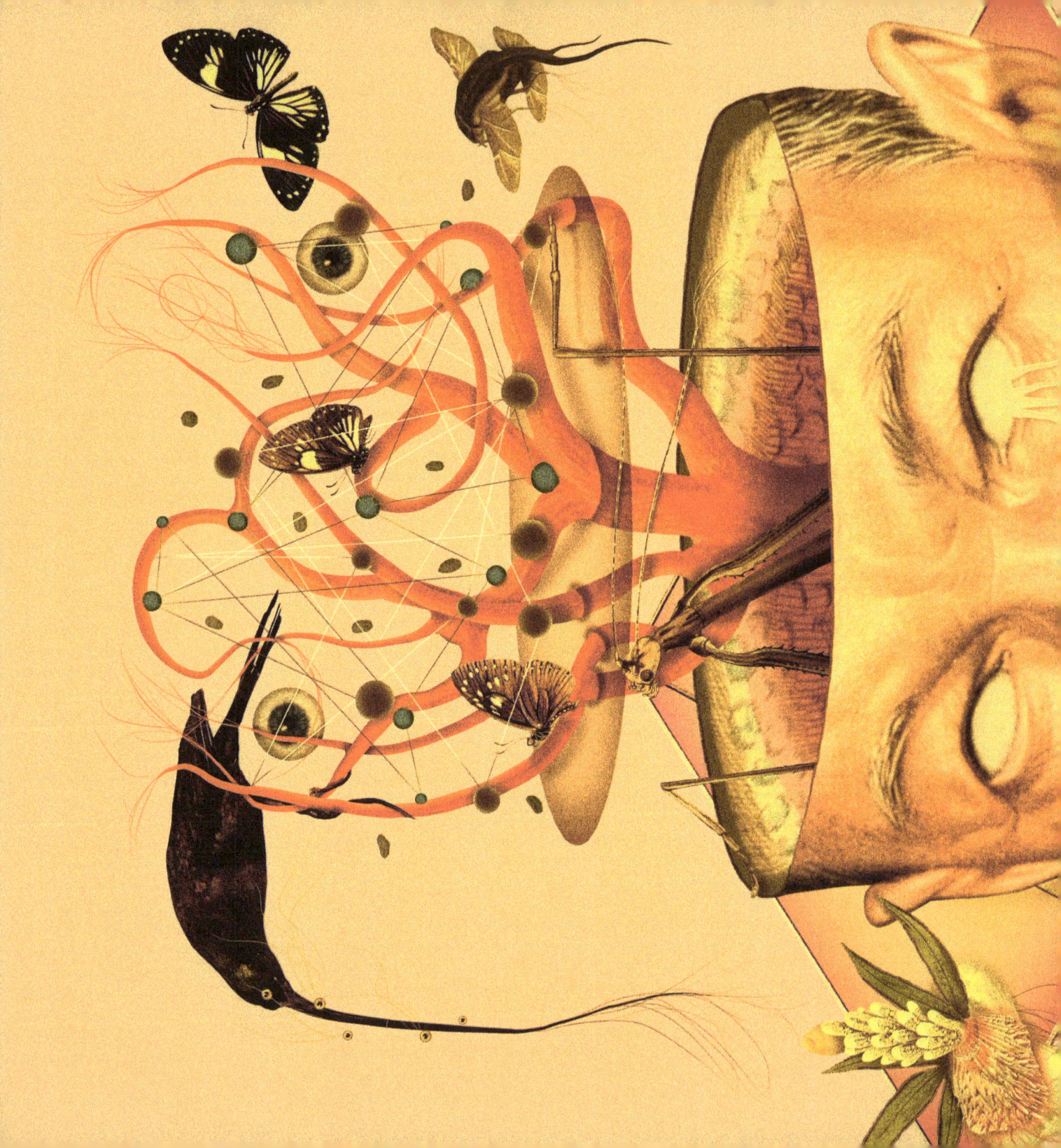

HOSSEIN EDALATKHAH / THE WOMAN / 2008

THE LIFE GROWING IN MY HAIR

My brain is burning
from the thoughts coming and going through my hair
there is a life in my hair
a life laying eggs
soon there will be a family
a community
a village of lice
in my hair
they will soon die from the sadness of thoughts in my brain

YING & YANG

If indeed there is a Ying and Yang
and if indeed every coin does have two sides
When do the two sides of a coin actually meet
It has to be when one side holds the other up to the mirror of truth

THE JOURNEY WITH NO MAP

There is no map
but there is a destination
there is no driver
but there is a guide
there are no plans
but...

MIDWIFE FOR LIGHT

I used to be a seeker
I used to be at times a beggar
But now I find I have only one role in life
and that is to be a receiver
Needless to say a receiver of light
a receiver of what can be done in regard to human rights
A receiver who does not know the meaning of collecting and storing
A receiver in flight
with sight
with almost no fright

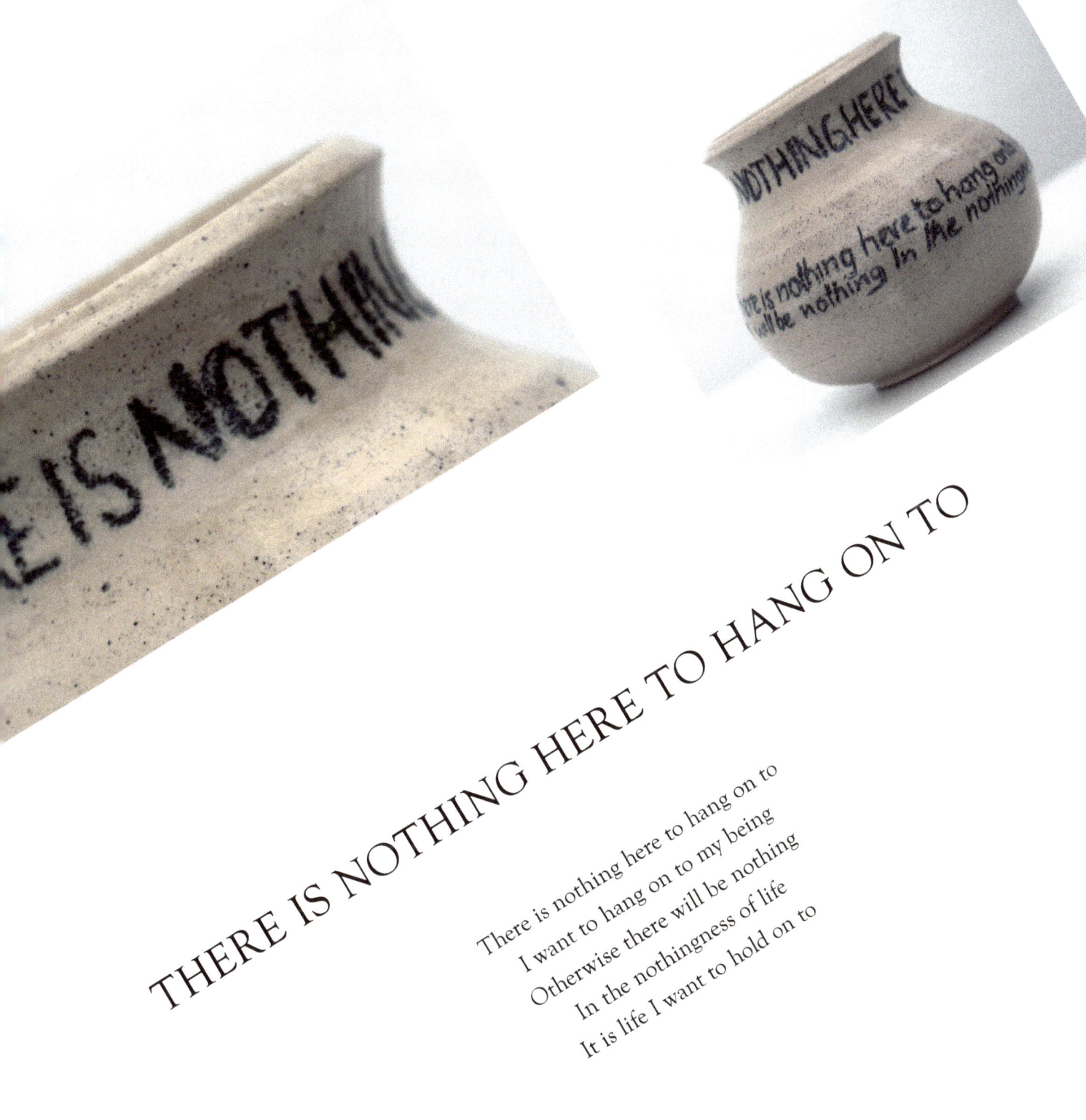

THERE IS NOTHING HERE TO HANG ON TO

There is nothing here to hang on to
I want to hang on to my being
Otherwise there will be nothing
In the nothingness of life
It is life I want to hold on to

I HAVE NEVER BEEN BITTEN
IN THE EYE BY A SNAKE

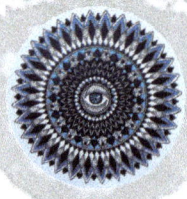

Sometimes I take my eyeballs out
and rinse them in the river
by which I sit on my rock
Each time I do the rinse my eyes are able to receive more light
I want to sit here forever
eyeballs
and river
and heart
receiving and shedding light

FADI AL HAMWI / THE WEDDING NIGHT / 2012
COURTESY OF EMERGEAST   WWW.EMERGEAST.COM

VIOLATION OF SOUL BODY & HEART

This is when I question the realities in life
Why must a woman bear a child and stay with a man who beats her while he moans
Why must a mother close her ears
as she hears the beating of her daughter's soul and body
her virginity taken from her under the same roof where no one lives
but her and the father of the girl
Why must the girl fall asleep
pretending that she does not know what just happened
A violation feels like a violation without being announced or acknowledged
Maybe these are the reasons why recently my eyes see all men in their naked truth
and all mothers at fault
There should be tenderness in the act of love making
There must be a purer love than what this father has for his child bride
The young girl will wear white on her wedding day
but she will bleed from inside on her wedding night
Bleed all her life for the family's sake
for the father's name

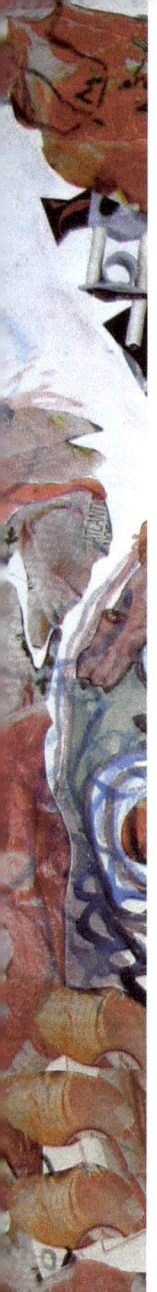

THE RAW TRUTH

When one thinks of Raw generally the image attached to it is not so nice
Raw sore
Raw meat
Raw eggs

There is however something incredibly pure and light about Raw Truth
The Raw Truth does not come in a fancy package with an orange bow on top
nor does it arrive in a carriage with 12 white horses and a courier dressed in black lace
The Raw Truth just arrives

Like the arrival of a baby after nine years of trying
This baby arrives passport in hand and cannot speak her mother tongue yet
The mother runs and greets her child
This is the sudden arrival of truth

There are other sudden arrivals
Like the day the father was digging the grave of his own son who had taken his own life
because he thought he had shamed his father by being born a homosexual
who is shamed and whose ideas should have been buried long ago

And who is to say what is the truth and who tells the lies
Not even in a confessional booth does the child tell his tale of rape by the priest to the priest
They both know the raw and painful truth of wrongful pleasures in the house of God

And the cold truth of being held in someones arms who feels nothing and pushes back your life
You give endlessly to the iceberg but the volcano that does not erupt leaves no ashes behind

I am alive in a vessel
The vessel is my body
Full of bones veins blood cartilage liver
lungs and all and yet this vessel is completely empty
Empty of desire empty of despair empty of knowledge
full of empathy and full of empty

ELMER C. DUCAY / MOTHER AND BABES / 2014

PEN & INK
Elmer Ducay
JULY 07, 2014
Filipino Artist

OH I'M SORRY

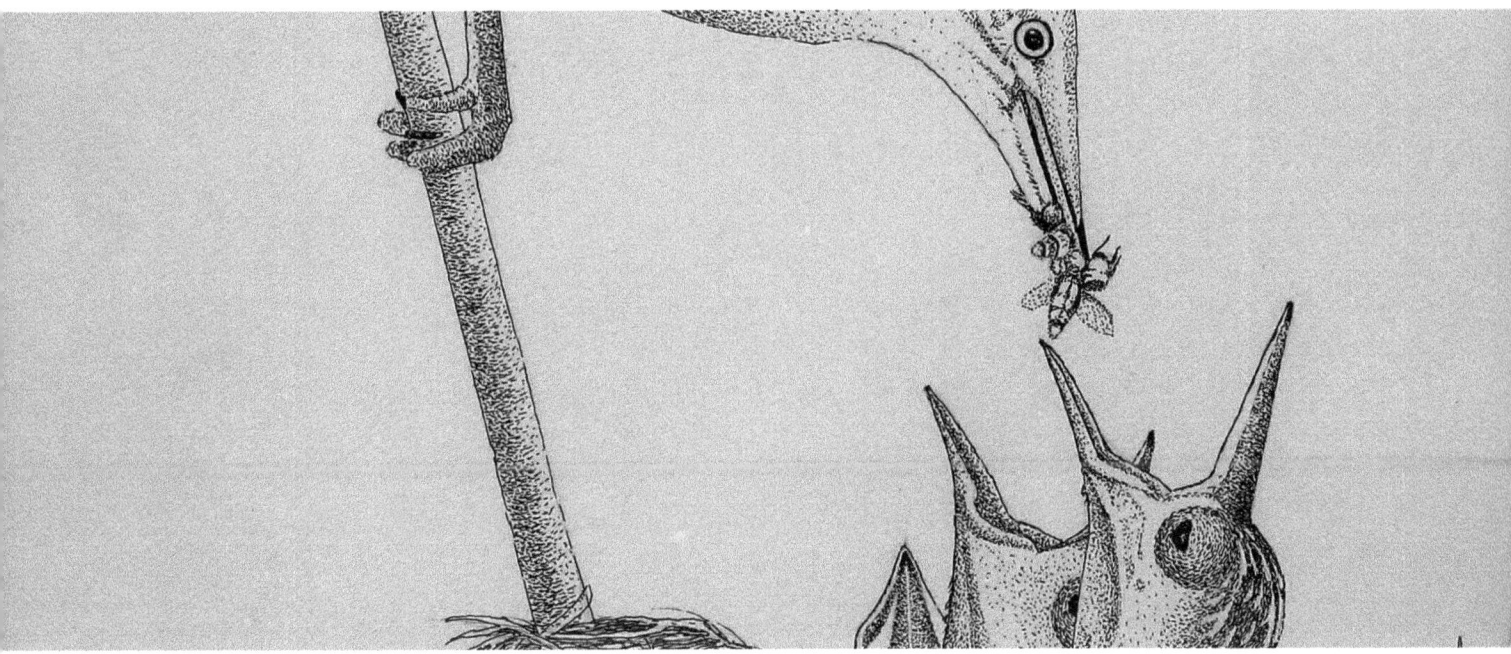

I remember meeting a lady about 3 years ago while watching our daughters swim
We shared a few niceties and then the question of how many children do you have came up
I noticed a small pause as she said three but my youngest has cerebral palsy
With out a breath or a thought I said you must be loved and you must be special
You were chosen
She looked at me with a beautiful smile and said that is the first time anyone has ever said that
The normal reaction is
Oh I am sorry
or not even knowing what to say
I say there is a reason for every breath and
there is a reason for our eyes to see

GROWING FINGER

Why is it that we cut hair and it grows back
Why is it that we trim nails and they grow back
However God forbid if a finger or a limb were cut away
it would never never grow back
in a day
in a week
in a decade
or in a lifetime
Hang on to your soul

ZARI JAFRI / SILENCE OF MY HEART / 2014

I HEAR THE SCRATCHING

I hear the scratching of my nails on the walls
of my heart from my inner core
I am a peaceful being and yet
I torment myself with the agony of my inner pain
There is a side of me
soft and gentle
pleasure to be around
And then there is the other side of me
I have met her on occasion
each time I pray I never meet her again

RULES OF THE JUNGLE

It is a difficult life if you want to speak the truth and
live by the rules of the jungle
Have you noticed animals don't kill just to kill
nor do they consume just to consume
They do not hoard or store things away
I thought we were animals
why have we lost all these beautiful animalistic traits
Now we use a linen napkin to wipe the blood of our own
kind from our mouths
We shame all other animals around

ONE WORD

This story all began in search of the one word that would make one not fall even if they jump
The one word must not differentiate between class and color
We are flying over a sea which holds the millions and millions of lives
of people who have jumped over the bridge of life
Does the sea carry the one word or is the sea the one word I seek
So we go back once again to the one word which would save a life at any time if in despair
The healing word which rescues a wounded heart and an empty soul
Do you know what this word could be
Yes indeed now I do have a sense
that there would be a truth in the word that gives hope and vision
That makes one forget the past and look ahead
With one instantaneous decision one is making all the past disappear
but even more so all the future to never appear
. If there were a person on a bridge trying to rid themselves of the realities of life
what would be the one word you would say
A word that would encompass Past Now and Future
A word that would mean hope without saying hope
A word that says look ahead and looking forward
A word with stability and no vulnerability
Yes the word is all-encompassing of what is light and bright to come
The word is
TOMORROW

I AM A ZEBRA WITH NO STRIPES

I notice individuals reaching into their briefcases
purses wallets and pockets

digging deep to find a small piece
of metal called a sim card

One carries his in a plastic bag

He has them in five different colors
and nationalities

She carries hers in a lipstick pouch
with a variety of flavors

I notice as each individual changes
the sim card in their phone

to match the continent and land which
they've landed in

They somehow change personalities
and their tone

Now I imagine people must carry hundreds of
those cards under their tongues

changing their views and ideas with every breath
and every no wind and no shine

My phone has no service and I carry no
alternative sim

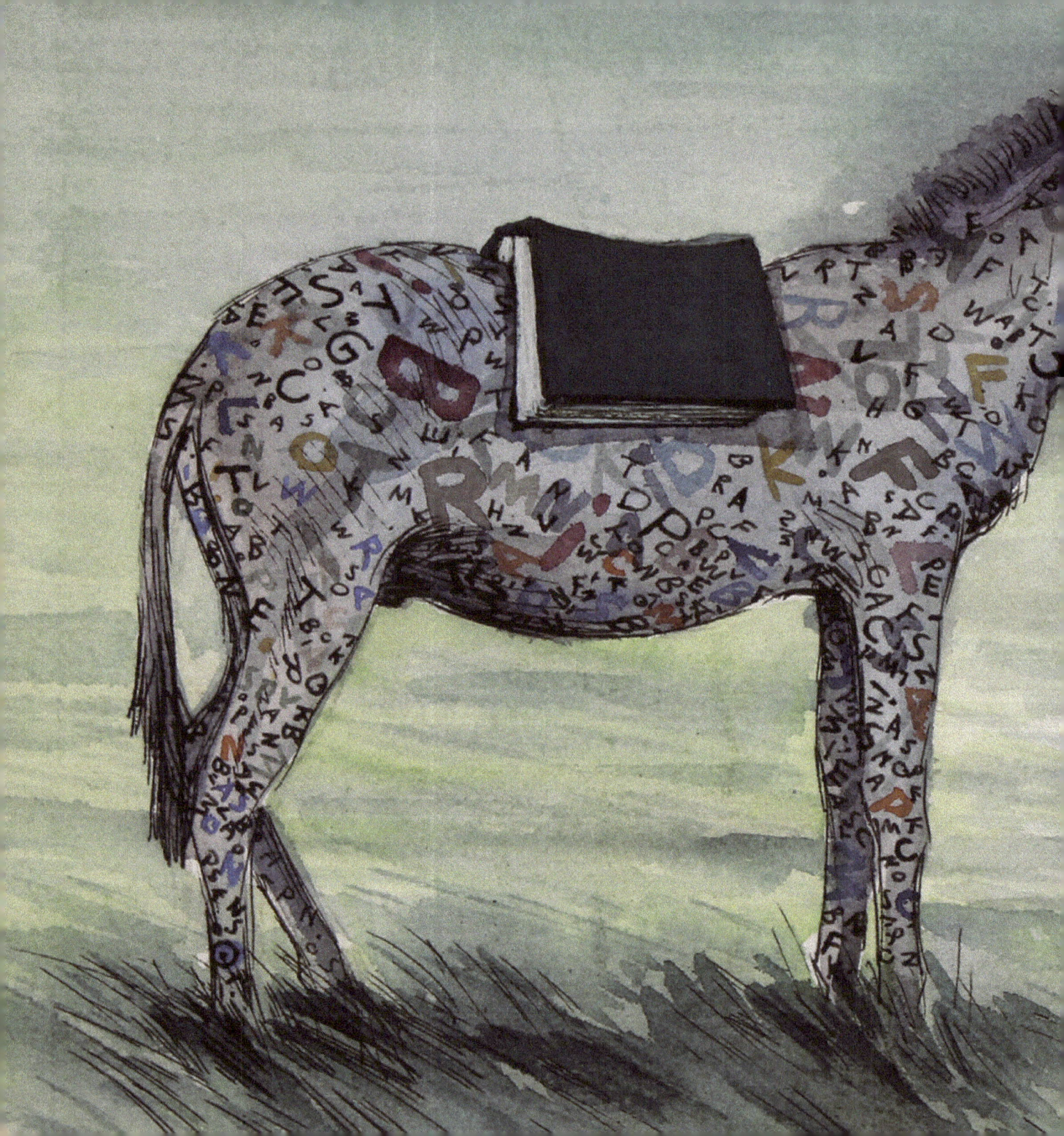

THE ELDERS SITTING IN THE KINDERGARTEN

Where have I been all this time
I have been looking for wisdom among the elders of town and sea
Today as I sit in a room full of respectful and respected souls with bodies around five years old
I realize wisdom and kindness comes in all shapes and sizes

The eldest of the group is a teacher over a few decades old
Her patience fills the eyes of every child's soul
She's reading a book about a fish called Big Al
but in reality she's guiding the children through the seaweed under the sea
She shows the children the tricks of the puffing fish
The energy and synergy
The respect and patience
welcomes individuality and growth here on earth

When all the kids get excited and start talking all at once
Each child's voice is somehow heard among the crowd
There is a lot of show and tell but also a lot of quiet guidance
without a vowel pronounced or heard
So many voices
So many listening hearts
So many wise souls

I hope with time I can become as wise as the one girl with the big pink bow
that lent me a smile and then took the hand of her teacher and went on her way
What a beautiful sight
This seascape

SULTAN

Sultan
The name of someone grand
I see a mother call her son
He is one born with Down Syndrome
But he will always be the king of the land for her
Her love is not negotiable
the syndrome of the child invisible

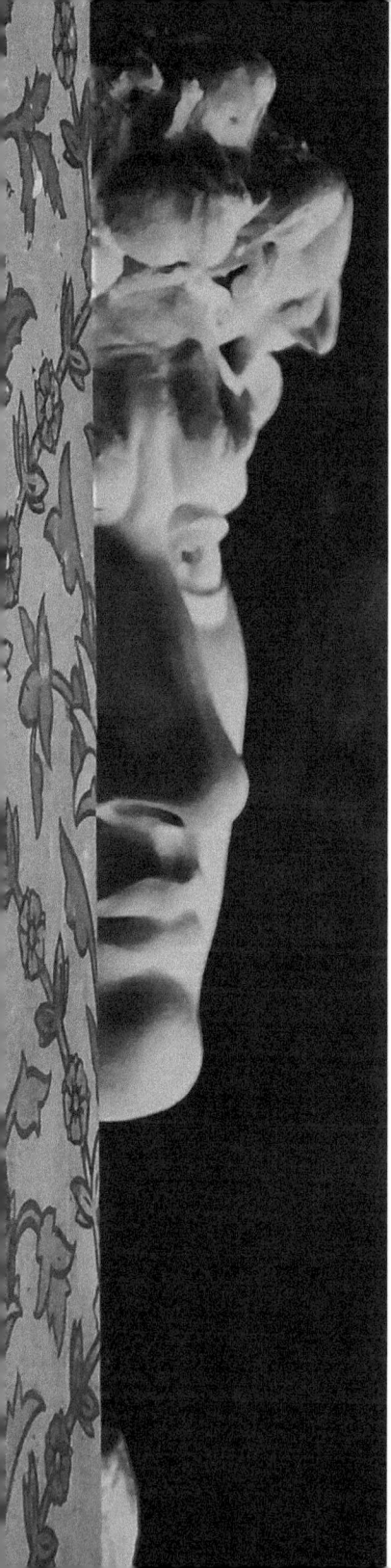

THE LOUD SPEAKER

The man standing in the middle of the square
is speaking loud
some stop to watch
some stop to listen
but there is no one
who sees or hears
the man on the box
A blind man is stopped near the box by his dog
The dog heard and listened
looked and saw
the man
on the box
in the middle of the square

THE CAMEL CARRYING WORDS IN HIS HUMP

Once upon a time there was a camel
This camel like many others traveled patiently in the desert
This camel unlike all the rest carried no water in his hump
He carried only words

Throughout the centuries as his ancestors had walked on the hot sands
and heard the tale of the traveling nomads
the words had been collecting
until the day the patient one was born
with all the words on his back

Carrying the words of brides and grooms
and also of the members of the clan carrying their dead to the grave
Carrying truths and lies
The same words carrying healing light and stabbing swords

The words of the ancient medicine men
and the words of the mama helping mothers give birth
The words of the warriors of life and also of warriors killing to remain alive

The camel carried sounds of cries
and the whispers of tomorrows that had not yet arrived
The camel carried the laughter of the young
and the despair of the old ones forgotten

The words carried carefully and tenderly and presently in the hump
Like seeds in gestation waiting to be watered given life through light
Even those words never spoken but only thought

All
All the words that have broken hearts and mended wounds
All the words that have started wars and ended lives
All the words full of life and no life at all

The beautiful image of the camel
walking through life with all the words in his hump
The reflection can be seen only in an oasis and in a moonlit sky

The words can only be seen by the ready and pure of heart
The language is universal
Every wise man and scholar can understand
but also each child not bearing a word on his tongue can feel

The blind man can add words to the back of his knowledge with his vision
The crippled man can add steps to the ladder leading to heaven
with his words paving the way

The deaf can hear the slithering of the snake on the sand
and without a word draw the poison out and release light

The dumb man can speak for a hundred and one nights
stringing together the words from the one humped camel
The beauty of such wisdom being carried in one hump

The same camel has carried thousands of journals empty of words
and also thousands of books with meaningless sentences upon sentences
trying to bring forth points of views
From all that the camel has observed only

The observations of the eye
The absorptions of the skin
The taste of the mist in the heat of the day
The sense of the touch of the sand on the hoofs
All carried

The presence of heart of the observer of Salat
The absent mindedness of the shrewd businessman carrying cold coins
The essence of being but not living all carried

All carried
All contained
All present
All omnipresent
The camel that carried the weight of all but left no footprints in the sand
All
Here
Now

All the words
All the wisdom
All the sorrows
All the joys
All carried HERE
Now
Ready to Deliver

SARA SHABANAZAD / THE FIRST OF INNER TURBULENCE / 2013
COURTESY OF EMERGEAST   WWW.EMERGEAST.COM

SNAKES IN MY ROOM

The wallpaper in the room is made from the skin of snakes
It is incredible to stand in the middle of so many snakes
and not to feel the venom of even one
One is an important number
Like the one chance one has to open one's parachute
The one fall that may destroy all grace
For me today the one belief I have in the one reason for my existence
gives me one mission in life
To stand in a room full of live snakes and to turn the venom of each one to nectar
one by one with love

I AM COUNTING

I am counting
Breathe in
Breathe out
God help me I was saying these words to myself all day
I should have seen her coming
The loud boisterous angry monster inside of me
Her name is mother
the same mother who held her babe
all night till the light of dawn
The sadness of the kind angry mother wanting to be held

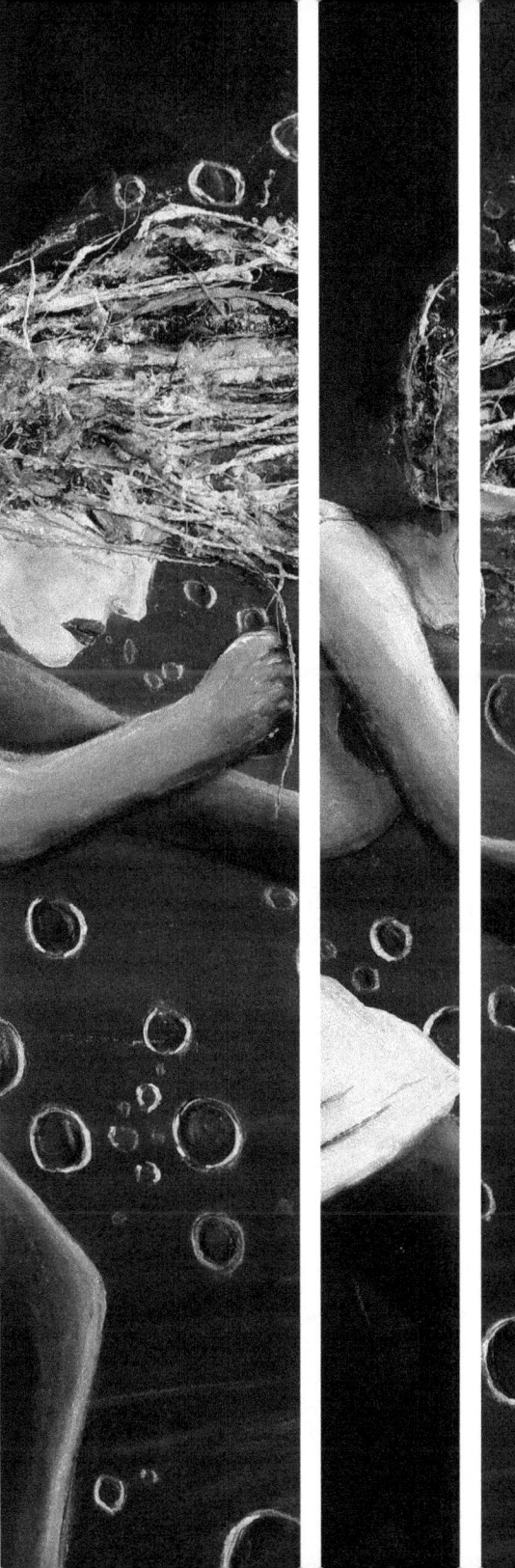

THE FLOWERS IN THE REFRIGERATOR ARE FOR MY GRAVE

We went to a building for lunch with the family called the new Souk
It is not the liveliest of places
The person with whom I share a bed said
it looks and feels like a state prison
I sat by the fountain in the courtyard of the prison
I had a few sentences to write to finish a pending thought after Friday call to prayer
My cellmate passed me by and mockingly asked what it is I do
I said I will finish and join you at the table of the feast
I did and when I thought it was time I announced to him and my daughters
that there will be times I will be called away
I will excuse myself for a few minutes
while I go to pray or write down some words that have come to me that I must capture before the
moment fleets away
I described it as one of his business conference calls that cannot wait
Everyone was quiet
my youngest daughter changed the subject to us changing our home in hopes of breaking the air

CORINA DEL CARMEL / THE DREAM / 2002

IF I COULD MAKE IT RAIN I WOULD

I realize I have no color
My faith is my guide
My religion is light
My call to prayer I hear 55 times a day
I drink the blood of Christ
And eat the body of every living saint
I hold and carry the rosary
As I walk around the house of Allah in the pouring rain
It is raining indeed
Raining with the glory of
God

PORCUPINE

When you think of a thorn
you think of a prick
When you think of a needle
you think of a drop of blood
Look at the needles on the porcupine
The needles are only a shield from the pricks and blood
Be careful
not to poke a heart
or bloody a soul

KAMILA ANWAR / ABSTRACT TREES / 2012

MOHAMMED AL HAWAJRI / WELCOME TO GAZA I / 2014
COURTESY OF EMERGEAST   WWW.EMERGEAST.COM

THE WHALE CRYING IN THE OCEAN

I see the baby deer sucking at his mother's milk
I realize everyone is milking the Earth of all it has
All the natural resources
the oil
the trees
and all that is under the sea
We are giving nothing back in return except for pollution of the air
the water
and even the desert
Our camels are dying from eating the empty plastic water bottles
The fish are choking on the oil
and the birds get their small necks stuck in the rings of plastic cans
I listen to the earth and I hear the whale in the ocean cry
He is crying from something he has swallowed
it is a combination of liquid nitrogen and mercury
The combination has made a fire in him and the smoke is covering the land

What will we tell our children and grandchildren and their grandchildren
when they ask us what a tree is
They will have heard of the name tree
but have no sense of what the shade of the oak tree feels like
and the bark of the eucalyptus smells like
We must protect their land
The land of our children and our ancestors

THE ACHING TOOTH

My tooth is hurting
it is not hurting from the sweet fruit of life
I took a deep bite into a rotten apple
bitter from the heart of the planter of the tree
I dug a hole beneath it
and buried my rotten tooth
Now the earth is aching
from the root of the tooth

I WANT TO LEARN TO FLY A KITE

Bahareh
Do you know what you will find
in you

A field of green with millions of butterflies
A sea of blue with yellow fish
A graveyard empty of bodies and souls for they are all at flight

In you
you will find with each breath in a sunrise
and breath out a sunset

How does that sound my child

I was asked by the light

I could not answer because I was all choked up with love

Can there be such beauty inside of me

I want to take my eyeballs out and put them in the other way

I want to look inward to the place of light

to the place of love

Such beauty in the simple truth of God

No searching

Just sitting

MOHAMED AL MAZROUEI / SELF PORTRAIT / 1989

ROPES HUNG FROM THE CEILING

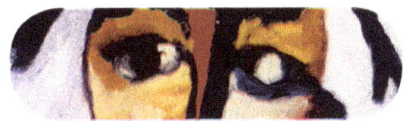

On the way home I noticed a brand new building being built
My spouse said there will be lots of restaurants opening there

My daughter asked if there will be a hotel to stay
All I was focusing on were the numerous ropes
that hung from the ceiling of the 3rd floor

They were all prepared for the people who wanted to hang themselves by the throat
I wondered if one would pay to enter such a destination
And would this be something one would do communally or one by one
Would the one that was hung already stay hanging for a while
or would the new one walking in take the cold one down

Some of them even had flowers under their feet
they had brought for their grave

For all this killing the odd thing is there was no blood shed at all

THE WRITING ON THE WALL MEANT NOTHING TO ME

It is as if I have woken up in a jail cell and I look around
to find out what it all means
How can it be that a princess in a glass castle on the clouds
would suddenly find herself in a cold damp cell
with nothing but the cold ground protecting her from the earth

I touch my legs and feel my warmth
Am I the princess in this story that cannot be considered a fairytale
but in fact the tale of a maiden's fall
I realize the reality of the situation
and I know I for one never believed in fairytales at all
The bleak realization of the truth pleases me
I smile but I do not cry

Just as I rub my eyes of the 44 centuries of sleep I have endured
I begin to realize that there is writing on the walls of the cell I am in
I find that the cell mates before me had each written a message on the wall

The first name I read is Nelson Mandela
then I recognize the frail hand of Gandhi
and the gentle handwriting of Mother Theresa
So many names so many eyes were here

The greatness of this moment takes over me
First I shiver like a person from a Tropical Island
who has found herself at the North Pole
Then I sweat as if a child with fever carried by Malaria with no cure in sight
After hours I touch my face in order to try to recognize the years
on my forehead
on my brows

I hear a growling I realize it must be coming from my stomach
I wonder how many sunsets have come and gone since I last fed my body
I feel my stomach and I assess that I carry extra weight and fat
Can it be the baggage I've carried around for all these years
Am I suffocating from overeating or am I in pain because of my vanity

I look around the room
Now that I have identified myself the cell feels more like a room
I see other names such as Hitler Stalin
and the man that stole from the beggar the other day

All these people saints in their own time to some but disliked by many today
There was a piece of advice from the good and the bad
Each saw the world with their own eyes and each left a mark

This cell seems to be a place
billions and billions of people have passed through
Some have changed the world for the better and others have made it worse
So many have passed through without a trace
Perhaps those are the ones that came to life
ate gathered drank and took a breath in but did not touch a life in any way
As I walk around the cell I touch each of the words and the people's names

I wonder why I'm here today
Am I on my way out to the world or do I have a foot in the grave
I realize that this awakening is like a second chance for me
It has taken me out of the glass castle and helped me see
I have the choice to go back into the glass castle on the clouds
and never leave a footprint or a writing on the wall
The decision takes no time at all

I spend hours and hours
weeks and months in the jail cell
as if a child in the womb reading the walls of the uterus
I too touch the walls and read the words I find that I am fed through

an umbilical cord which extends through the window to the light
I am connected to the world
I am connected and the earth is impregnated with my force and energy
I am ready to come alive

I know I do not want the glass castle on the clouds
After studying the millions and millions of writings on the wall
I feel the answer in my heart
I know that I will offer something unique to the world
I will not be a saviour of one land or one religion
I will not only work for women's rights
I will be the rainbow bridges connecting sky to sea
East to West
And faith and light to all

And as I ponder I know that one day my name will be on these walls
I see an empty space somewhere between Hitler and Gandhi
and there I see rays of light
Sometimes people fear the word of God
But they may embrace the warmth of a sun filled sky
The message comes from that warm place
connecting the cell even to the castle in the sky

C. B. HARKREADER / WOMAN THINKING 1 / 2010

THE SPIDER BITES

I just saw a woman pass me by
A beautiful person inside and out
I just cannot begin to realize why her face is covered with spider bites
I have heard of the kiss of a spider
I would not anticipate kisses could leave such marks
Oh but it occurs to me what if in another life she was victim of human trafficking
and her soul and her face were kissed by the poison of one buying her
I now know what it means to say
Don't sell your soul

VULTURES PREYING

All the vultures stand around ready to eat the game that was hunted by another
They know that it is food but they wait for it to be carved up
Carved up not like thanksgiving turkey
But more like carving up what was once their father's
who left no will

ARIANA SHARGHI / CARVED / 2015

NIRINA ROLANTO / NEW CALLIGRAPHY / 2015

MY HEART IS CALLING OUT WHO IS LISTENING?

The tablets on the bedside table are all the same color and shape
From time to time I take one to sleep and then another to wake
If only I could fall asleep so fast to the realities of life
Then maybe I would not lie awake night after night

FLOWERS IN THE SUN

Have you ever
looked closely at a sunflower
look look
with each seed
comes a story
of the journey of a soul
the light of the soul comes from within look inside
look inside yourself
look inside the sunflower
and look for the glowing soul

LANRE OLAGOKE / THE TREE OF LIFE / 2012

SASAN NASERNIA / WINGS / 2016

IF ONLY WINGS MEANT FLIGHT

If only wings meant flight
I would walk across the land
and follow each migrating clan of birds
in search of any feathers dropped from the sky
If only wings meant flight
I would visit every corner of dark caves
to see if bats have left a dropping
With each sign I would travel deeper within
in search of flight

If only silence would teach me to listen
I would crawl back into my mother's womb
and listen to her lullabies
If only silence would teach me to see
I would wear blindfolds of many colors
and those colors would tell me the meaning of words
not spoken but heard
Listen

If only wearing white was the sign of one ready for pilgrimage
I would paint my skin white
and cover myself with all the white feathers I had found
and I would wait for the call to prayer
And for my reception to be held as I entered the
House of Me

If only after a walk in the desert
each drop of sweat left behind would mark my place in life
I would go back at night with a lantern and read
all the maps and the plans
my plain eyes could not see in the day
I can see in the dark

If only words meant meaning
I would collect all the dictionaries in the world
and string the words together in prayer
I would wear the strings of words around my neck
in hopes of finding meaning in what people say but don't mean
Am I deaf or dumb or just not blind

If only the word love meant

all the wonderful things hallmark cards make the word to mean on Valentine's day

If only Valentine's day would be dedicated to hate

and all the other days of the year to love

Love would mean Peace

If only Peace was

not only a sign we would make with our not one

but two fingers raising

And if Peace was not depicted as a rainbow

or a bird carrying grace

Then peace would be felt when eyes actually meet eyes

in greetings that would constitute a prayer

And Prayer
What to begin to say of Prayer
If only we would just abandon all the crosses
and crescents and the stars
If we would leave the houses built for prayer that are being bombed
Then in our own solitude
in our own temple
we might light a candle and herein Pray

And if only chandeliers made of diamonds
lit with electricity or candles of bees wax meant light
Then I would carry a kerosen lamp
and travel home to home turning on light
Light is not to be turned on or off
Light is ignited
There is a call
There is a spark when lovers meet

If lovers were to be depicted
as man and wife
or man and man
or woman and she
The world would be full of lovers
But somehow there is an essence
in Thee-and-I and
I-and-Thee
This essence is the most romantic relation of all
All accepting
All encompassing
All Love

WITH DEEP GRATITUDE...

Thanks to the artists

To all the artists who have trusted me with their art in this collaboration.
Your work has brought "The Carousel of Life" to life.

CHARLIE DAVOLI / SPAIN

Remember the day I told you even if you give me a blank piece of paper I would be happy? That day you spoke to me of illuminated beings. Thank you for helping the Angel find his flight. May you always carry truths and capture hearts through your art.

www.instagram.com/charlie_davoli

MOHSSEN KASIROSSAFAR / IRAN

A chance trip to Rome, a chance walk with a dear friend to your little street. She heard the music and was drawn in. Yes the rest is history, she a photographer, I a poet. You a musician, photographer and poet. I like seeing the world through the reflections on water you capture.

www.instagram.com/musettaluna55

HANNAH SHARGHI / USA & IRAN

You have been with me through many oceans, more importantly through so many waves. I am fortunate to have you as an equalizer. Your voice, your words, your art and your being. Thank you for bringing your artful self to this moment now.

ZARINAZ MOTTAHEDAN / IRAN

It was just an encounter, meeting you, getting to know the lunar calendar and the solar movements through your knowledge. Getting to know the purple hues of your art is like listening to the music of my own heart. I am sure your art plays this role of music to the heart for many near and far. I thank you for this tune.

CHRISTINE SPRING / NEW ZEALAND

Serendipity is what brought us together on that day. You were presenting your lecture on serendipity and I was mesmerized by what the lecture was bringing to life each moment. Thank you for visiting the Emirates with me through words and images of yours. And here now I raise a hand and another and I add joy to life thanks to you.

www.christinespringphotography.com

PIERRE SCHMIDT / GERMANY

I wonder where the detached heads have all gone? Are they in reality looking for a deserving soul? What a great depiction you have presented Pierre. I will come to you to find the right match if ever I see my head detached from my soul. Continue creating such wonder.

www.dromsjel.de

ANITA DE RAAFF / HOLLAND

From being a top-level corporate executive to a creator of jams and mosaic realities, you are the person that remembers the first day of spring and has arranged going to a concert to hear songs. Through you I am listening more to the music of my heart. Thank you.

HOSSEIN EDALATKHAH / IRAN

If only you had not shown me your wings, I would not have believed such an Angel could live here on earth. You carry with you many wings, and you help others in search of flight. At this threshold I met you and herein lies the story in my head.

www.hosseinedalatkhah.com

ABDULLA AL MUHARRAQI / BAHRAIN

The forces of nature are much like the forces of colour. Your art has made the balance come alive. Through the power struggles in life, one comes to find a space between breaths. Thank you for the light.

www.emergeast.com

SEEMA MANOJ / INDIA

You and I met in a classroom in a school with a wonderful teacher and students. You, through your open heart, have captured my essence in words on paper and now as poetry on pottery. Thank you for this vessel that carries light and truth.

SAI RAHUL RAJU & SAI ROHAN RAJU KAKARLAPUDI / INDIA

You are indeed young, but your art has the soul of many lives. I am fortunate to have met you on this journey and to have shared this part of it with you. I wish you all the success in the world. As you well know success is measured only in colours and strokes. Enjoy.

http://goo.gl/LnrbNK

ANNA MARIA / MALAYSIA

How magical to make an image with henna and also into something permanent and sublime. Your art is so intricate it invites the viewer to look within for answers. The eye is the core of what helps us see, and of course the heart must be open to sight. Your gift brings this reality closer to life.

www.instagram.com/4nn4henna

LINDA HOLLIER / SOUTH AFRICA

Who would have ever thought that I would have found a friend and travel companion for life as I was learning to tweet. Thank you for not only retweeting my first tweets, but for being with me each and every step as I start to find my way from here2here.

www.lindahollier.com

FADI AL HAMWI / SYRIA

The beginning of each relationship is tricky. So was yours and mine. We have not met yet in person but my words have found a home in your colors and mind. The depiction of truth captured by you. Each person will always see his or her own side. I see inside out. And you?

www.emergeast.com

ELHAM ETEMADI / IRAN

There is a truth to all stories and that truth can, at times, be raw. Who would have thought that your art depicting raw meat would bring flight to the story hiding to get light. Thank you for seeing beyond the here and now and helping me see through the lies.

www.emergeast.com

ZARI JAFRI / FINLAND

The simplicity and beauty in which you capture peace and truth speaks to me. Your heart, the moments we have sat together in a sacred room bring peace to my heart. Thank you for allowing me into your heart.

www.instagram.com/zarikaarinajafriart

ELMER C. DUCAY / PHILIPPINES

A slow walk in the neighbourhood brought me to the window at which you were drawing. Your lines, the detail in which you draw and paint shows the connection you have with all things alive and not in the world.
I am glad to be connected with you.

www.instagram.com/elmerducay1024

EDA DURUST / TURKEY

Some truths are hard to write about, some truths are hard to speak about, and you with your art, both write and speak of truths unspoken. May there be reality and life in all that you represent. Thank you for being with me on this journey through jungle and life.

www.edadurust.com

RICHIE MONTGOMERY / USA

How does one start to count on one hand the beauty of life? It is through your fingers that came this beautiful art divine, and through mine that came the words in search of the light. Thank you for being on this journey with me.
Let me start counting one, two, three...

www.1-paul-montgomery.artistwebsites.com

ALIREZA DARVISH / IRAN

Yes, it is true, we did meet through a mutual friend on Facebook, but then when I started looking into your art, I started to become intoxicated with the truth told in books through your art. Thank you for encouraging me so much to make this happen. The orange, the zebra, the fish, the carousel....

www.alireza-darvish.com

FARZANA FATIMA NAEEM / INDIA

Where does one begin, to say that I have seen you take your first steps would be true, to say that you have given me strength as I have taken my first steps into the world would be true. Dear Farzana, know that no matter where I am in the world, auntie is waiting for you and will be at the door to greet you…. as long as you promise not to scare me with your tricks.

www.intheparktoplay.com

FARIDEH ZARIV / IRAN

First it was your smile that captured my heart, the smile that was only a reality of the heart that glows from inside out. The camels in the desert have found the words I need to bring to the world. I am grateful for your art and I will continue to watch your flight.

www.faridehzariv.com

EHSAN MAJIDI AHI / IRAN

When I was writing the story of Sultan I never knew that there was such strength waiting for me. The strength behind the image not complete, the dots not connected and yet the power shown through and through. Deep gratitude for the throne for our Sultan.

SARA SHABANAZAD / IRAN

The incredible thing is to know I am on one side of the world and you on the other and yet we both imagine the same snakes in the room, mine in words yours in colors and strokes. Thank you for this connection from dream to reality to here and now. See you in my dreams.

www.emergeast.com

NASSER PALANGI / IRAN

I met you once in the desert where there were no camels. There you were making creations with left over metal and other junk. Gratitude for your vision to bring "Up-cycled" to life, and your gentle ways of opening doors to people's hopes for tomorrow including me and mine.

www.nasserpalangi.com

AMIRA ABURIDA / USA & EGYPT

You know you are so much more to me than my daughter's friend. You are the artist who speaks out loud through her colours and strokes. I admire your strength and your kindness both of which have helped me grow.

www.instagram.com/amiraaburida

CORINA DEL CARMEL / MEXICO

Through your eyes, I begin to see another dimension. One that is real but not seen, one that is real but not heard, one that is seen by you and now I begin to see. Thank you for exploring this other dimension and for letting me in on your journey.

www.corinadelcarmel.com

MOHAMMED AL HAWAJRI / PALESTINE

There are many doors in the world. Some open, some closed. And through your art I am able to start looking where I may never have seen. The whales hope to stop crying and I hope to start seeing life through an open door even when there is no door at all.

www.emergeast.com

HANAN AWAD / PALESTINE

I never knew a simple trip could fill one's heart on so many levels. Thank you for taking me to Palestine to plant olive trees. Those seeds will grow at the depth of my heart always. Grow and enlighten and fly.

www.facebook.com/hanan.debwania

YOSRA MOJTAHEDI / IRAN

Yosra, the light in your eyes balances some of the dark depictions that you are able to capture for others to see. Thank you for capturing even a toothache in a way felt by me, by the person eating the apple under the tree and by the universe.

www.yosramojtahedi.see.me

KAMILA ANWAR / PAKISTAN

Dearest Kamila, who would have thought a simple Google search, would have brought us together. I am grateful for this meeting, and for all the depth and breath that you bring to my life, to the world.

PETER SKÖLD / SWEDEN

I came walking down the hallway in the hotel in Abu Dhabi where you were exhibiting your art. The colours directly went into my soul and I started to write. Thank you for inviting me to share my words at your opening. Your art here in this book is an opening to conversations between me, myself and I.

www.pskold.com

MOHAMMED AL MAZROUEI / EGYPT

From the union with writers to the union of friends. It is you that can see beyond words and yet beyond the art with no words. I am thankful for your friendship and for always helping me start to think and question that otherwise would pass me by.

www.mohamedalmazrouei.com

LAILA SALARTASH / IRAN

Remember "The Moment"? Yes, we discovered you paint in the moment and I write in the moment. Over the years I see your art and I see the Presence in each stroke and each line. Thank you for sharing this journey with me.

C.B. HARKREADER / USA

Dearest Christine, you arrived at my doorstep one early morning in the form of an email. Thank you for looking into my words and finding a space of light and color. Deep gratitude for your depiction of the poetess of Light which will carry me forth. The fish in the ocean will always speak to me through you, as will the scars on the face unseen unheard.

www.cbhark.com

ARIANA SHARGHI / USA & IRAN

The truth is that there is no carving, nothing has been carved, but yet you can capture so much in words painted on walls. You can also capture so much through your open heart and mind. I am blessed to have you in my life.

NIRINA RALANTO / FRANCE & MADAGASCAR

I find that it is only a person that understands the language of the universe that can create a "Universal Language". Whether I am awake or taking a pill to fall asleep I will remember there is a travel companion that sees this universal truth.

www.nirinaralanto.blogspot.ae

LANRE OLAGOKE / ENGLAND

Dearest Lanre, the story of how we met is beyond belief, but now that I have gotten to know the core of the artist behind "The Tree of Life" I know there was a reason for this meeting. You are a guiding Light.

www.instagram.com/lolagoke

SASAN NASERNIA / IRAN

Thank you for meeting me on this part of the journey period. Your strokes and colors have helped my words find flight.

www.nasernia.com

WITH DEEP GRATITUDE...

Thanks to those who have helped make this book come to life

Saghar Moayeri for her creative creation, patience and wisdom as she weaved the words and the art together and really helped give flight to "The Carousel of Life".
www.sagharmoayeri.com

Nikki Meftah and Emergeast for her trust and artistic contributions.
www.emergeast.com

Miriam Ahmed Hanafy for her support, kind and gentle edits.

Special thanks to Gleb Osipov for his brilliant and creative designs
www.glebosipov.com

Special gratitude to those who have shed light on my poetic journey

Special thanks to Farah Joon, my dear sister who was the very first person who listened to some stories I had written in Farsi and asked me "when did you start writing poetry"?

Raz Moinzadeh for being a mirror and helping me see myself and hear my words.
Thank you for being the first person to help me listen to my own words and help me realize I am a poet.

Sonya Eldelman who first heard my voice and acknowledged my words, and made the effort to make videos to capture my poetry.

Hana Makki for sitting with me for hours and making such incredible poetic productions, such as Speak Abu Dhabi.

Farrukh Naeem whose vision and insight and expertise
in social media have made this journey filled with Light.
You have always seen beyond where I am now and indeed to where I will be going.
www.farrukhnaeem.com

Dr. Diane Harvey who has been a guiding Light on my journey for the past 30 years. Thank you Dr. Harvey for being my teacher for years. Thank you Diane for being my friend always.
Your questions always help me find my way home.

GRATITUDE...

There are no words to thank my family...

And of course this book would not be possible without the daily support of my family:

Thank you to my daughters Ariana and Hannah who are the lights of my eyes.
Thank you for showing me what true love means. I have felt so held and loved by you.
I hope I can somehow help fluff your feathers as much as you have fluffed mine.

And most of all to my husband and companion in life Emad Sharghi
for supporting me through all of the words and the silences.
Without your gentle love and support I could not make this happen.

BIOGRAPHY

Dr. Bahareh Amidi is a poetry therapist who believes words and voice can be instrumental in the healing process for people of all ages and backgrounds worldwide. She has spent many years in the Middle East working with youth, victims of human trafficking, women in safe houses, and men in labor camps. She also has worked in the Silicon Valley with groups of high tech professionals and business executives working for international companies.

Dr. Amidi grew up in the USA and currently is based in Abu Dhabi, UAE. She holds a Masters Degree in Family, Marriage and Child Counseling Psychology from College of Notre Dame and a PhD in Educational Psychology from The Catholic University of America. Dr. Amidi completed her post-doctoral Certification in Poetry Therapy at the California-based Institute for Poetic Medicine.

She regularly holds poetry sessions, workshops and seminars for poetic expression and healing in communities, schools and universities in the Middle East and the United States. Dr. Amidi also has shared the tremendous potential of Poetry Therapy on the prestigious TEDx platform with people from all over the world.

Dr. Amidi believes in offering "poetry therapy in a capsule." The common factor is always a piece of paper, a pen and a way into the heart. The results are often revealed immediately: a teardrop, a flash of insight, or a smile--the beginning of a self-sustained journey on the path of healing.

A FEW WORDS ABOUT...

The carousel spins and spins and at the center of all spinning, contains a deep and profound steadiness, a quietude. Poet Bahareh Amidi, with "all...collected in (her) heart" invites us to contemplate the depths, the expansive horizons of being, with awareness and care. Consideration dwells everywhere, belongs to all. "With every step my heart goes in twice as deep as last year..." - pause. "I would love to be in the heart of a dog" - stretch. Her giant soul suggests we too may revel in the visual delights of her pages and our days - no one is exempt, or disqualified. "I would spend some times in the mines where people are trying to find themselves" - she would shine a light, by seeing more and more. And what do we find in this style of thinking? "The more I see my smallness the closer I feel to you." World community. Connection. Relationship.

Could anything be more crucial, now and always? This book is a gift.

*

Naomi Shihab Nye
Poet, Songwriter, and Novelist

"Bahareh is a stellar human being.
I greatly admire and feel grateful for
the healing spirit of her poetry and the
compassionate work she is doing."

*

John Fox
Author and Certified Poetry Therapist

"*Carousel of Life* by Bahareh Amidi is truly an inspirational journey that bridges the gulf between East and West. So profound in its intensity, you will be propelled to search deep within your own heart in an ageless yet deeply personal and incredibly moving universal quest for truth."

*

Laura Sims
Poet and Retired Nurse

"In the poetry of Bahareh we find
a woman whose searching words are –
that rare treasure – beyond time and place.
Her words speak to the heart."

*

Esther de Waal Ph.D.
Author and Benedictine Scholar

Are her poems
Like stars
Lighting up the still dark sky?
No, they are more.
Her poems are like
Rare comets
Carving the heavens
With knives of light.

Hearing them, we forget.
For such a precious moment,
Even to breathe,
But when we do,
We are happy
In a way that
We do not fully understand.

Thank you for
What you have
Already done
And for so much
That you will do to make this future
World kinder,
As flowers soften hearts.

*

Jim Fadiman Ph.D.
Psychologist and Writer

Thank you dear readers, dear travel companions for coming with me on this part of my journey.

If any part of this book touched you in any way; if a poem made you happy or sad or if a topic resonated with you or irritated you, I would love to hear from you.

You can always contact me at connect@bahareh.com
Until we meet again soon.

Truly and always
InLight
Bahareh

Listen to The Carousel of Life
www.bahareh.com/carousel/

Book Details ISBN The Carousel of Life
ISBN: 978-0-9974573-0-8 (hardcover)
ISBN: 978-0-9974573-3-9 (paperback)
© Bahareh Amidi. The Carousel of Life. 2016. All Rights Reserved

connect@bahareh.com • www.bahareh.com
facebook.com/BaharehAmidi • youtube.com/BaharehLIVE

I would like to close with honoring those who are no longer on this carousel with me at this time, especially my father who believed everything is possible and helped instill the same belief in me and my dear brother, Hamid, who was ahead of his time and always put the needs of others before his own.
I feel your presence with me always.